Town of Vienna

Historic Images

A Bicentennial Celebration: 1807 – 2007

by the Bicentennial Committee
of the Town of Vienna

Published by

Town of Vienna
North Bay, New York

North Country Books, Inc.
Utica, New York

Town of Vienna

Copyright © 2007
by the Bicentennial Committee of the Town of Vienna

ISBN-10 1-59531-014-2
ISBN-13 978-1-59531-014-9

Design by Zach Steffen & Rob Igoe, Jr.

Front Cover Photo: The Elmira, Cortland & Northern Railroad station in Vienna

Library of Congress Cataloging-in-Publication Data

Town of Vienna : historic images : a bicentennial celebration, 1807-2007.
    p. cm.
  ISBN-13: 978-1-59531-014-9 (alk. paper)
  ISBN-10: 1-59531-014-2 (alk. paper)
  1. Vienna (N.Y. : Town)--History--Pictorial works. 2. Vienna (N.Y. :
Town)--Social life and customs--Pictorial works.
F129.V63T69 2007
974.7'62--dc22
                            2007034735

Published by

Town of Vienna
2083 State Route 49
North Bay, New York 13123
http://townofvienna.org

North Country Books, Inc.
311 Turner Street
Utica, New York 13501
www.northcountrybooks.com

CONTENTS

Acknowledgments...v

Governmental & Public Buildings..1

Fire Departments..5

Churches...9

Schools..17

Military...27

People...33

Farm & Home...43

Business & Manufacturing...53

Hotels & Restaurants...75

Fire & Storm Damage..89

Roads, Bridges, Rails & Canals...101

Recreation..117

Bibliography...129

ACKNOWLEDGMENTS

We extend our sincere gratitude to everyone who loaned their pictures so this history could be compiled. In addition to loaning irreplaceable material, people shared stories and memories with the compilers.

Ann Hopkins shared her wonderful collection of postcards. David and Doreen Weeden shared connections to the Seventh Day Adventist's church archives. The Queen Village Historical Society also shared their archives. Descendents of John I. Cook shared their family history archives. We would also like to thank:

Martha Norton Wilson	Joseph and Carol Bator	Donna Merriam
Kathryn Hutchings	Michael Fitzmaurice	Kathleen Holmes Tilton
Michael and Penny Milliken	Aaron Eckel	Shirley Herder Boardman
James Ott Jr.	Calvin and Ruth Collins	Diane Alvord O'Rourke
Arthur and Shirley Sable	Lorna Eckel Cable	Robin Haskins
Joanne Ziemba	Norman Kirk	Marie Dixon
Harriet Snyder	Ron and Ellen Turk	Lois Drought
Rose Pounds	Rita Fern	George Cook
Henry Stagner	Phoebe Lacell	Ethel Eckel Palmer
Rita Dixon Moring	David and Sue Montroy	Anne Teelin
Harold Woodcock	Carl Eckel	Pearl Reising
Mary McCall	Todd Groves	Robert Collins
Louis Brown	Ella Meinen	Mary Jane Clifford

Several members of the bicentennial committee worked long hours to share, compile and edit material. We can never thank them enough.

Nancy P. Fusco gathered photos, stories, and publication releases for the project. Nancy also planned the layout. Arlene Flagg shared her own records and gathered much more from others who volunteered assistance. Brandyann Phelps scanned and organized photos, and wrote text. Nancy P. Fusco, Marilyn Holman, Karen Washburn, and Penny Milliken edited text. Bob Montross shared his remarkable memories and photos. Betty Carpenter organized the material into chapters and edited the text flow. Stephen Carpenter donated his graphics experience to organize and export all the files for publication.

Special recognition goes to Mary K. Brown (deceased) and Bob Montross, both Town Historians, and Elaine Clarke Norton (deceased). They have been exemplary gatherers, sorters, and writers.

Rob Igoe, Jr. and Zach Steffen of North Country Books have guided the Bicentennial Committee through this project.

All above are commended for sharing their love of local history.

GOVERNMENTAL & PUBLIC BUILDINGS

The Vienna Town Hall and office building, erected November 1973, was made possible through the efforts of the town board: Supervisor George Harrison, Town Justices Arthur Sable and Gilbert T. Rogers, Jr., Councilmen Edward Stewart, Sr., and Laurence E. Montross, and Town Clerk M. Dorothea Kinney. The building was dedicated June 2, 1974.

The Sylvan Beach Municipal Building, ca. 1920, had a court house and trustees' rooms. Bob Montross recalls entering by the side door for Boy Scout meetings that were held upstairs in the 1950s.

The Grange Hall at Jewell, ca. 1920. This building stood west of the Hall Road intersection and on the lake side of Route 49. While the Grange has always been a private organization, it has indisputably influenced rural government.

Rose Pounds & Ella Meiner

The place where Pine Road, Oswego Road, and Herder Road converge is the heart of the hamlet of Pine. The first Blossvale Post Office was established here in July of 1832, with Joseph Filkins as postmaster. In the late 1800s to early 1900s, this same building was a stagecoach stop and coach exchange called Five Corners Hotel. The third floor was a dance hall. In approximately 1923, the third floor was removed and the building was sold. It has been the home of Frank and Nettie Kimball, their son Arthur (Esther) Kimball, and granddaughters Pauline (Mrs. Donald) Wright and Ella (Mrs. Robert) Meinen.

Around 1956, the first Sylvan Beach Post Office (shown ca. 1900) was transformed into the Pancake House. Moe LaBella owned and operated the restaurant, a popular gathering place for locals and tourists. After forty-nine years, he retired. It is now operated by a direct descendant of James D. Spencer, founder of "The Beach."

Once the McConnellsville Post Office, this building, shown in 1908, was also the home of Theodore Chrestien, partner in the Tuttle Canning Factory.

FIRE DEPARTMENTS

On March 24, 1914, the Sylvan Beach Volunteer Fire Department became a member of the New York State Firemen's Association. The department incorporated on July 23, 1915. In 1927, a fire district was formed. In 1951, a building next door was joined to the original station, and in 2000, it was remodeled to look as it does today. Here it is shown as it was in 1955.

This Fire Station, built by North Bay firemen, is shown in 1932 with North Bay's chemical truck. The men shown, left to right: Chief Clayton Montross, George J. Johnson, president of the fire company (seated in truck): Russell Phelps, secretary and treasurer, and William H. Allen, vice-president.

Nancy P. Fusco

Bought as army surplus for one dollar in the mid-1940s, this 1942 Dodge Power Wagon became an irreplaceable part of the North Bay Volunteer Fire Department. Requests to use the truck for off-road fires are often received from other fire departments.

The Vienna Volunteer Fire Department, pictured in 2001, is housed on Route 49.

Glen (Pete) Lacell in the Vienna Volunteer Fire Department ladder truck in 1950.

In 1936, a class "C" fire department was organized in the village of McConnellsville. The Frank S. Harden Company volunteered the use of their garage to store the first truck, a used American La France fire engine. Incorporated on January 13, 1950, the fire department continues to contribute to the community by teaching fire prevention and CPR classes and offering various functions for children.

CHURCHES

The Vienna Methodist Church on Route 13 in Vienna was the town's earliest noted congregation. In 1804, Circuit Rider William Keith from Baltimore, Massachusetts, came through the area, preaching in small town barns and schools. A small class was formed in Vienna. In 1837, the land on Route 13 Vienna was purchased and a church was built. In 2003, a new Methodist Church was built about a mile down the road on Route 49, and the church building on Route 13 was sold.

Built in 1887 on land donated by James Spencer, the Union Chapel of Sylvan Beach was begun by parents who wanted Christian education for their children. Its walls lift open for lake breezes or close for warmth and comfort. The chapel still serves Sylvan Beach every summer, and local Protestant pastors conduct the services.

Father Mertens, born in Brussels, Belgium in 1861, was the priest of St. Mary's on the Lake Roman Catholic Church when it was built in 1899. Located across Main Street from Eddie's Restaurant, it was the first Catholic Church in the area. It closed in 1965, replaced by a larger and more modern sanctuary south of the canal.

Sts. Peter and Paul Roman Catholic Church on Mulholland Road was built in 1843 on land donated by Major Mulholland. It was west of the cemetery.

In 1939, the cornerstone was laid for St. John's Roman Catholic Church on Route 49 in North Bay. The land was donated to the church by Peter Loftus after his home and barn burned in April 1926. In 1958, the church was designated the mother church for the area.

Methodist Church—North Bay, N. Y.

The North Bay Methodist Church, built in 1879, was an active part of the community. It closed on December 31, 1969.

Sue Montroy

The North Bay Methodist Church Sunday school class, each member dressed in fashionable Sunday-best, posed beside the church in 1929.

The North Bay Baptist church was built in 1862 by H. J. Meyers. Active for many years, it later became the Odd Fellows temple.

Until this Maple Flats Baptist church was built in 1902, church services were held in the nearby schoolhouse. The first pastor was Yates Ford, a Civil War veteran and pastor to other Baptist churches in the region. He also supervised a large dairy farm at his home and was a road commissioner and supervisor for Camden for a time.

In 1878, the West Vienna Free Chapel was established on Route 49 in Jewell (West Vienna). As a meeting place for all religions, it was built through the hard work and cooperation of local citizens. To raise funds, they held socials, plays, musicals and excursions on the lake. The projected cost to build the chapel was $399.20. In 1886, the Ladies' Aid built a steeple on the little chapel. The chapel was closed several times through the years. In the spring of 1917, it was included in the North Bay charge along with Vienna. Rev. Charles Fulton was the full time salaried pastor for all three churches. In 1921, the village and the chapel changed their name to Jewell. In 1988, a certificate of incorporation for the Jewell Baptist Chapel was filed with Oneida County.

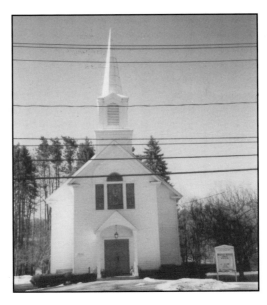

The McConnellsville Community Church grew from the early Methodist Episcopal Church at the McConnell farm community. In 1918, the Methodist Church was struck by lightning and burned to the ground. In 1920, Frank S. Harden retained the services of Mr. William Beaven to supervise construction of a new church, assisted by Chester Tanner and Charles Palmer. The building was completed in 1921, and it became a community church in 1923.

Mill Street building, 1899

New church, 1961

New school

In 1899, the Seventh Day Adventist congregation bought a former saloon on Mill Street in Vienna to be used as a church and school. Land purchased in 1957 enabled groundbreaking for the new school on Eckel Road in 1957 and the new church in 1961 on Route 13. The congregation is still active in the community, although the school is no longer used.

SCHOOLS

The Stone School House was built in 1848 on the corner of Route 49 and Pine Rd. in Vienna.

Stone School students, ca. 1950. Front row, from left: Barbara Loomis, Joe Mundy, David Coates, Roger Loomis, JoAnn Deeley, Gloria Plopper, Melvin Deeley. Back row, from left: Victor Kimball, Lauren Loomis, Arthur Kimball, Joyce Plopper, Peggy Plopper, Junior Towne, Sally Coates, Richard Lattimer.

Pearl Reising

Pine Road School students, on Oswego Road, in 1937. Students pictured include: Orin Hilts, Earl Stagner, Albert Lacell, James Stagner, Jason Hilts, Donna Hoffert, Ken Stagner, Howard Wright, Gene Teelin, Raymond Hilts, and Wesley Teelin.

Pearl Reising

Six Pine Road School boys: Howard Wright, Albert Lacell, Wesley Teelin, Pete Lacell, Raymond Hilts, and Donny Wright, proudly rode their bikes on picture day.

Joseph A. Cook was an early trustee and clerk in the Fish Creek Landing School (District #18). His notes from an 1845 annual meeting of voters speak of repairs on the school and furnishing the school with wood for heat, so we know there was a school building before the one pictured here, built in 1869. In 1901, after closing the Whiskey Island School, School District #18 became School District #16. In 1950, it was absorbed into the Camden Central School System.

Fish Creek students on a slide, 1942. From left: Shirley Harrington, Carol Young, Mary Ann Cable, Doris Woodcock, Shirley Hilliker, Jeannine Brown, Verena Eckel, Matilda Spencer, Audrey Hilliker, Leona Chilson, Alma Cable, Marietta Relyea, Louise Spencer, Lorna Eckel

North Bay Elementary School had two classrooms. First through third grades were in one room, and fourth through sixth grades were in the other.

North Bay students on October 4, 1948. From left to right: First row: R. Dunham, L. May, unknown, B. Yager, D. Clapper. Second row: F. Baker, M. Granger, R. Clapper, R. Montross, unknown, N. Phelps, R. Dunham. Third row: G. Eastman, M. Dunn, Mrs. Wells (teacher), L. Yager, R. Collins. Fourth row: R. May, G. Griffen, M. Andle, C. Taylor

This school at Jewell was built after 1860. It stood near the Grange Hall at Hall Road, near one of the many streams flowing from the north shore into Oneida Lake.

Lorna Eckel Cable

The Eckel Road School at Vienna was constructed ca. 1910–1914.

Students at Eckel Road School. Front row: Clayton Raut, unknown, unknown, Dorothy Saddler McGraw, unknown, James Saddler, unknown. Middle row: Alice Beeman (teacher), unknown, unknown, Madeline Saddler Peacock, Frances Dora Brown Loomis, Ruth Saddler Ripka, unknown, Harriet Saddler Hooper, last four unknown. Back row: unknown, Viola Peck, Beech Eckel, unknown, Mary Elvira Mott Brown, last four unknown.

New two-room school—
McConnellsville, 1906

Union Free School District
Students—ca. 1906

The trustees of the Bailey District, the McConnellsville District, and the Annsville or "Brick School" decided to consolidate districts into a Union Free School District, located in McConnellsville, in 1906.

23

Built in the 1800s, the Maple Flats School was also used for church services.

Maple Flats School students and their teacher, ca. 1955. Front row: Teacher Mrs. John Davis (Elizabeth), Charles Worden, Stewart Worden, Jean Taylor, Ruth Garlick, Pauline Garlick. Back row: Henry Phelps, Robert "Jim" Taylor, David Garlick, June Treen, Frederick Marshall.

The Dibbletown schoolhouse was built sometime after 1860. For decades, local children were taught within its walls. It closed in the mid-1900s.

Dibbletown children and their teacher, Miss Loomis, in 1910. Front row: Effie (Warner) Allen, Guy Congden, Inez (Phelps) Preston, Asa Warner, Doris Tuttle, Arthur Tuttle, Marion Hooper, Charles West, and Ernest Barnes. Back row: Marjorie (LeClear) Joslyn, Miss Loomis, Ida (Dibble) Deeley, James Barnes, Mark Congden, and Ruben Dibble.

MILITARY

In October 1915, Civil War veterans gathered in Washington, D.C. to commemorate the fiftieth anniversary of the end of the Civil War. Pictured standing is Casper I. Cook, born and raised in Fish Creek Landing. He lived the remainder of his life in North Bay.

Boy Scouts at Memorial Day exercises in North Bay honor those lost in war. The Memorial Monument was completed ca. 1955. The inscription, taken from a poem by Laurence Binyon, reads "At the going down of the sun, and in the morning we will remember them." Listed on the monument are: Ernest Faulkner, Arthur Becker, Lawrence Werthman, Patrick Flanagan, Clarence Towne, Frank Francisco, Raymond Adams, Wilfred Holmes, and Kevin Forbes.

Fighter Pilot Charles (Bob) R. Strader, son of Mr. and Mrs. C.R. Strader, was inducted in 1942 in the Army Air Corps. Shot down by a Japanese gunboat in the Makassar Strait miles from his base, he lay in a partially inflated raft under a cloth sail and did his best to hide from the enemy. Japanese search parties came within feet of Strader several times, but he was rescued the next day by a Catalina flying boat crew. He later married Betty Redner.

Lt. Arthur K. Becker, son of Alfred and Gertrude Becker of North Bay, enlisted in the infantry. He was lost in battle at Guadalcanal in 1943 and is buried in Arlington National Cemetery.

Taken Nov. 1943

Second Lt. Patrick J. Flanagan, son of Albert and Elizabeth Flanagan of North Bay, enlisted in the Army Air Corps. Patrick was an engineer on a cargo plane that went down over Burma, India, and was never recovered. He was posthumously awarded the Purple Heart.

Richard Kinney served in the army in Europe in World War II and was in many notable battles there.

Commander W.J. McClanathan of Fish Creek, a descendent of William and Martha McClanathan, has continued his service within the community.

PEOPLE

Jack Henke

James D. Spencer (1813–1899) was born in Amsterdam, New York. He came to this area in 1840 and is considered the founder of Sylvan Beach.

Elaine Norton

Elmer J. Clarke
1845–1928

Elaine Norton (1918–2007) exhibited steadfast devotion to the Vienna community. An avid historian, the value of her contribution to this project was indisputable. She is greatly missed.

Albert Brown and his wife, Dora, were proprietors of the cheese factory in Vienna.

The stone house located at the west end of Swartz Road was built in 1904 by Elmer J. Clarke, a Civil War veteran. Elmer was born in 1845 in Middleport, New York, near Hamilton. He enlisted in the Civil War in 1862. His stepmother said that he couldn't go unless his father went with him, so they both went. They fought for a year and returned home safely.

Elmer had always wanted to live in central New York, so around the turn of the century, he moved his wife and nine children to the location on Swartz Road. He used the skills he acquired as a stone mason to build the house. Elmer died in 1928 and is buried in the North Bay Cemetery.

The house lay empty for a few years before Elaine and Roger Clarke Norton decided his grandparent's homestead would be a fine place to raise six children. But first they had to renovate, remodel, and add indoor plumbing. In the process, they found the stone walls of the house were two feet thick, consisting of an outer wall and an inner wall with gravel in between. They also found a sealed glass jar placed in the wall as a time capsule. It contained the Clarkes' Civil War discharge papers, along with several other items.

Andrew Young was a fisherman in North Bay. Pictured here in 1899 or 1900 with his houseboat, he found full-time fishing employment nine months of the year.

Clayton Montross is shown at his gas station and auto repair shop in 1954. Clayton's father, Ed Montross, owned the last blacksmith shop in North Bay. Clayton converted the shop to serve automobiles. One of the first auto mechanics in the area, he was well-known for his quality work.

James and LaVanche Raut lived in North Bay. He was town clerk for a total of twenty-four years. His wife, LaVanche, worked beside him as an appointed deputy for many of those years and eventually became registrar. James was first elected in 1919 and served for eight years. Andrew Miller and George Johnson would hold the post over the next ten years. Elected again in 1937, James served until he retired in 1953. He was held in such high esteem by both the Democrats and the Republicans they urged him to run again, but he refused.

Jack Kinney (1920–1991) was an avid outdoorsman who loved hunting and had a large collection of antlers in his garage. However, he grew tired of the "road hunters" that drove by his home. Seldom entering the woods, they just drove around and shot at deer through the car window.

Jack Kinney

Jack showed his wit and ingenuity when he built a bogus deer using a set of antlers, a sawhorse, some hay and a tarp. Placing it in an open field among the tall grass, he sat back to watch. He didn't have long to wait. A car screeched to a halt, the driver lowered his window and reached into the back seat for a rifle. As he began blasting away, Jack's deer stood unaffected by the barrage of bullets. The driver continued firing until the gun was empty. Reloading, he left the car and walked up to the deer; even from a distance you could see the man's face turn red.

The next driver used a different tactic. Easing his car to a stop, he quietly left his vehicle to stalk his prey, crawling on his hands and knees across the field. Halfway to his destination, the man jumped up and shot repeatedly at Jack's deer, which continued to stand unscathed. There were many more episodes like these, but you get the picture.

While some may question the validity of this story, the people who knew Jack know it's true.

The C.H. Loomis triplets were born October 23, 1885. They were a rare marvel.

Vienna News.

LIVE AND LET LIVE.

VOL. III.   VIENNA, N. Y., SEPTEMBER 6, 1879.   NO. 1.

Vienna News Survives as Chicken House

The birthplace of the *Vienna News* was located on Route 13 between Vienna and McConnellsville. William Bowman was twenty years old when he began the newspaper, which was published from 1877 to 1881. A quote from the young editor shows his sense of humor; "If you see a mistake, let it pass and remember your editor is only a boy." A subscription for the *Vienna News*, a four-page, sixteen-column weekly newspaper "sent to your address," cost just fifty cents a year.

William Bowman was a bachelor living with his parents, and the newspaper was conveniently located in a building across the street. On April 1, 1881, he moved his newspaper to North Bay. Through the urging of Dr Cavana of Sylvan Beach, he moved to Oneida a short time later. While there, he established and successfully published the *Oneida Post* for several years.

A skilled musician, his love for music led him away from the publishing business. He taught music for a while and then partnered with Howard Janes at North Bay, forming the North Bay Cornet Band. For a number of years, the Bowman and Janes Orchestra was in great demand.

Bowman and Janes moved to Cleveland and opened a photography business. Bowman's home and the building where he published the *Vienna News* was later owned by Mr. and Mrs. Edward Phelps.

Taken from an article by Mary K. Brown (historian, deceased)

Historian Mary K. Brown peers in the Vienna News office, ca. 1950.

Charles Harden, Sr., (b. 1828) was the son of Henry Halstead Harden (1797–1860) and Sarah P. Harden (1797–1879). In 1862, Charles Harden Sr. and his family permanently settled near the McConnell farm along Fish Creek. Three years later, he bought the old John Halstead sawmill and began a lumbering business. His son Frank joined him and soon added a general contracting business. In 1884, the Frank Harden Company, which started out with eight or ten employees, built their "first solid chair." In 1902, the Frank S. Harden Company was incorporated.

Frank S. Harden was born in 1858.

His wife was Olive M. Harden, born in 1863.

William and Martha Abbott McClanathan built their house, the first in an area north of McClanathan Avenue, with the help of relatives. The four McClanathan brothers, Francis (b. 1863), Charles Lester (b. 1857), Elmer (b. 1861), and John Henry (b. 1859), farmed an area located near Sylvan Beach and marketed their produce there. A large farm with forty-five milkers, it was a full time job for the brothers. Fish Creek provided drinking water for the stock and irrigation for the 524 acres of meadow and pasture. For years that area was known as McClanathanville.

George Barton Herder holds his son Ernest Eugene. George bought a farm in 1899 from Fillmore G. and Catherine E. Utley. Ernest began running the farm with his father in 1928. They raised foxes and chickens. In 1974, the farm was sold to George and Marcia Gafner.

Shirley Herder Boardman

40

Kathryn Hutchings

James and Arlene Murray. James, son of William H. Murray, served as the Supervisor for the Town of Vienna for several years.

Clinton Drum, the last rail master in Jewell, is shown with his wife, Stella.

Jay and Eleanor Ischia began their wagon repair and fabrication business on the family farm in Blossvale in 1943. Managing their farm by day, they repaired farm wagons and trucks after hours. Over the years, their business grew from welding and repairs to all things automotive. Jay and Eleanor led the rotary, volunteered their time, and donated money to community projects.

Wes Teelin of Blossvale (front right), December 1952. Though primarily a dairy farmer, Wes exhibited many other talents and interests, such as his band "Wes Teelin's Orchestra." The band played "Big Band Swing" and square dancing music and was popular at many local gatherings, parties and proms. During the 1940s, '50s and '60s they often appeared on Friday nights at Beck's Grove in Rome and at Pete Howell's restaurant in Sylvan Beach.

Nancy P. Fusco

Historians Bob Montross and George Cook are pictured on the occasion of George's 100th birthday on October 7, 2006. Both are known and respected for their ability to share local history and life stories.

FARM & HOME

The Stone Barn at Stone Barn and Elpis Roads, Jewell, was built ca. 1900 by Charles W. Knight, a civil engineer from Rome. He called his creation "Eralaust," a name he derived from the letters of his family's names: "Er" came from Erma, Knight's wife; "al" from Alta, his mother-in-law; "au" from Arthur and "st" from Steward, his two sons.

Knight kept forty-four to sixty Jersey cows. Each cow had a drinking fountain fed automatically from a spring brook via windmills and a manger built of stone and concrete.

Beautiful living rooms were along the front of the upper floor, and there was a private room where Charles conducted personal business. The building was heated by two large furnaces, and a ventilation system carried away impure air. He raised his own corn, but other grain and hay had to be purchased.

The barn was cleaned twice a day, and the ceiling, covered with wainscoting, was washed quite frequently by hand. At milking time, each man was required to take a shower and put on a white suit. The cows were not able to lie down during milking, and their flanks and udders were carefully cleaned.

The milk was taken to a milk room, strained, and then sent to the bottling room. Only one man was allowed here, where milk was cooled, bottled and iced before delivery to the Ontario and Western Railway station. The "certified" milk was transported to New York City hospitals, hotels, and homes. They also made one-pound blocks of butter stamped "Eralaust Farms," which sold for one dollar.

Mr. Knight abandoned his project before World War I. Construction costs nearly exhausted the engineer-dairyman's funds, and actual operation of the farm failed to realize any profits.

A fire destroyed the roof and wood interior in 1946, leaving behind only the massive stone walls.

From articles by Mary K. Brown, a former Town Historian, and Carrie Hoover Harris

44

Art Neiss and his uncle, Ray Neiss, are shown with their hunting dogs. Fox pelts are hung in the background. Often the income from these pelts paid the taxes on their farm.

Willard Teelin, his son Wes, and father-in-law Hub raised as many as a thousand turkeys a year during the 1930s and '40s. Willard won over 300 ribbons and prizes for his bronze turkeys from as far away as Harrisburg, Pennsylvania, New York City, and Boston.

Lewis Eugene "Gene" Holmes and Bessie Humaston Holmes established their farm at the corner of Yager and Eckel Roads, Vienna, before 1900. They raised dairy cows, hogs, and chickens. The first barn burned, and the present barn was built in 1929. Their eldest son, Lewis Holmes Jr., bought a farm of sixty-five acres on Yager Road from Royal Yager in 1938. He and his wife raised five children on this farm and then sold it to Lauren Stedman after they retired. Gene Holmes is shown with oxen, ca. 1951–52.

The Herder farm was purchased in 1899 by George B. Herder. He raised chickens and foxes for fur and meat. The fox venture ended in the 1940s. His son Ernest joined with his father in 1928 and after George passed away in 1949 he became the sole proprietor. The five hundred acre farm was sold to George and Marsha Gafner in 1974.

Ruth Garlick Collins

Charles Garlick and his son Raymond owned a farm about two miles north of Cleveland in Maple Flats. Four acres of that farm were devoted to strawberries that kept the family and neighbors busy for four weeks each year in June.

Michael Fitzmaurice

The Dixon homestead, Dixon Road, North Bay, in 1910. Appearing in this picture are: Jim Dixon, Hubert Covell with his sons Ben and Edmond Covell and daughter Agnes Covell. Benjamin Murray, a veteran of the Revolutionary War, and his wife Lucretia Ranny Murray, bought the farm in 1814 from Cornelius Ray. Their daughter, Lucretia, and son-in-law, William Williams, lived with them and inherited the farm. When William died in 1867, Lucretia sold the farm to John Dixon and his wife, Mary Jane. The property has descended down through the Dixon family.

Founder of Har-Phel Farm, Harley R. Phelps, shows a prize-winning bull in 1923.

Harley's son H. Russell Phelps shows another 1923 prize winner.

Harley R. Phelps and Jessie Cook Phelps were married in 1901. Within a year Harley began working his farm, which consisted of three properties: the "Yager Farm" located on the corner of California and Yager Roads, the "Clark Farm" on Littlefield Road, and the home farm in the valley, North Bay. His son Russell stopped farming around 1960, but he continued to tell people he was a farmer until he passed away forty years later.

Stagner farm, Oswego Road, Blossvale

William "Earl" Stagner with Kit and Jenny; Jimie Sunday in background, ca. 1935. The barn on the left burned May 18, 1943. William Stagner and Nettie Reinhart were married in 1893 and lived on the Stagner farm until 1900. Their son, William Earl Stagner (who was born on the farm in 1896), also operated a blacksmith shop and took care of the stagecoach horses. Donald, Henry, and Kenneth Stagner took over in 1972 and continue to run the farm.

Stanley Turk and son Ron on a John Deere tractor, 1951

Gathering hay on the Turk farm, 1951

Purchased in 1940 by Harrison and Elsie Turk, the farm consisted of 482 acres. Harrison raised beef cattle and milked approximately sixty cows. Their son Stanley sold 305 acres to Ron and his wife Ellen in 1987, making it a three-generation farm.

The Cook farm (later the Grenholm farm) on Cook Road, Fish Creek, in 1910

Clifton "Cliff" Collins shown with his four sons in 1950. Left to Right: Calvin, Raymond, Floyd, Cliff, and Roger. Cliff Collins created the name of his farm by using "Gren" as a shortened version of Green and adding "holm" which means "fields by the water." Calvin and Roger inherited the farm from their parents, May and Cliff. Calvin and his son James Collins own and operate the farm today.

Louis Brown

During the 1800s, John and Phila Halstead occupied the Halstead homestead on Blossvale Road, Blossvale. It was handed down through the family and eventually sold. The property had dwindled from several hundred acres to the six acres Louis Brown bought in 1966.

Cornelius Van Woglum built the Woglum-Flannagan homestead on Mullholland Road, North Bay. In later years he dropped Van from his name. By 1906, Mrs. M. Flannagan acquired the property. Today, a portion of it is the home of the Oneida Pines Campgrounds.

BUSINESS & MANUFACTURING

Ann Hopkins

This old basket maker was located in Sylvan Beach. The postcard was created ca. 1900.

Several potters were located on Murray Brook, which crosses Route 49 and divides the valley in North Bay, and one was situated at the mouth of the brook where it enters Oneida Lake. The first pottery business was established in 1848 by Peel H. Webster. After two slow years, he partnered with Symmis Bergen, a local doctor. Their stoneware mark was Webster & Bergen/North Bay. In 1850, Henry Williams built a pottery. His kiln produced earthenware and in later years, only flower pots. E.H. Farrar arrived in 1851 from Geddes, near Syracuse, but only stayed a short time. His pottery mark was E.H. Farrar/North Bay. Lastly, in 1851, John C. Waelde, a craftsman from Willenburg, Germany, arrived in North Bay. Unlike his predecessors, John settled in and stayed for twenty-five years. His stoneware was particularly appealing because he decorated his pottery with brush and stencils.

Looking north in Vienna, 1913. The Albert and Dora Brown cheese factory is on the left and Meay's store is on the corner. Note the railroad runs between the two businesses. Pictured on the wagons are: Isaac Kent, Eugene Wheeler, Ben Cook and William Deyo. This was the main street of the hamlet of Vienna in 1913.

Here is a rare look inside the cheese factory in 1922.

Hubbards Mill in Dibbletown, 1907. People lived, struggled, and achieved in this little hamlet a mile or two north of McConnellsville, but we know very little about them. Dibbletown was located in the present-day area of Elpis and Dixon Roads. Anyone that lived in Dibbletown has long since passed on or moved away. We do know the town had a saw mill, a canning factory, and a school.

Ann Hopkins

Mace's Grist Mill, West Vienna (Jewell), 1906

Ann Hopkins

Mace's mill in later years was owned and operated by Claude E. Harris.

Kathryn Hutchings

The eight year old boy seated above the flour on the wagon is John Harris, brother of Kathryn (Harris) Hutchings. West Vienna (Jewell), 1922.

A poster advertising Union Mills, owned by C.E Harris.

The old paper mill was located on Fish Creek at the west end of Teelin Road in Blossvale. The road was originally called Sand Hill Road, later Paper Mill Road. The Blossvale Paper Mill Company was formed in December 1906 when seven acres were purchased from Fred Wyker and Minerva C. Wyker of Liverpool, New York. A dike was built to power the mill. T. Joseph Foley of Rochester, New York, owned the mill in 1920; he changed the name to Foley Paper Mill. On December 22, 1924, Mr. Foley declared bankruptcy and the stockholders relinquished all rights and properties. Then William McKenzie purchased the company. The company changed hands several times over the years, and finally Frank Harden and John Halstead purchased it. Descendants maintain the property to this day.

The blacksmith shop on Route 13 in Vienna, ca. 1915, was owned by Frank Chilson. To its right was a wagon shop.

Frank Chilson at his blacksmith shop, ca. 1915

Charles Harden Sr. and Son (Frank) produced kitchen chairs. The first kitchen chair they sold was built on June 1, 1884.

Clarence Harden

In 1862, Charles Harden Sr. settled in McConnellsville. Three years later he bought a saw mill from John Halstead and began a logging and lumbering business. Shortly after, Charles and his son Frank added general contracting, and that led to manufacturing. By the end of the 1880s, their company was building homes and other buildings in rapid succession, along with furniture. In 1884, C. Harden Sr. and Son Company built its first "solid chair" and employed just eight to ten workers. Producing these two types of products eventually became overwhelming, and they split the company into two separate businesses. Charles Sr. continued with the lumbering business, while Frank took over the furniture business. By the turn of the century, Frank's business had grown so much that in 1902, the Frank S. Harden Company was incorporated, with Frank Harden as president and Charles H. Chrestien as vice president. Charles H. Harden Jr. (Frank's eldest son) was secretary/treasurer. In 1970, Clarence Harden wrote that "The Harden Furniture Company is the largest employer in McConnellsville, manufacturing 300 designs of fine wood furniture that is sold all over the United States."

Journal of a Village / McConnellsville, N.Y. 1828
by Clarence C. Harden

The Harden mill dam

The Harden store in McConnellsville, 1930. The Harden Furniture Company remains a leading producer of fine furniture and is a major employer in the area.

Ann Hopkins

The Lewis Miller home on West Lake Street, North Bay, in its early years. Some years later, the building was remodeled and opened as Lock's Store.

Bob Montross

Through the years, the building that housed Lock's Store served as a gas station, grocery store, post office and funeral parlor.

Bob Montross

The McCormick Groceries & Dry Goods store, located next to the Methodist Church, was the first store in North Bay. It was owned by Nicolas McCormick (1846–1902) and his wife Francis (1853–1925). It is shown here ca. 1880.

Bob Montross

Dr. Willse used the same building years later as an office and drug store. At one time, it was also used as a Christian Science meeting house.

Ann Hopkins

In 1873, Frank Harden joined with others to build a three-story building on the northwest corner of what is now Route 13 in Vienna. It is shown here as it looked ca. 1908. On the first floor, John Henry Meay operated a general store that also served as the post office. Mail was carried by stagecoach at that time. The second floor contained a large room with a stage used for entertainment. The Methodist church performed skits here as fund-raisers. On the third floor was another large room used as a meeting hall for the Masonic Lodge and Order of the Eastern Star. Dr. Charles F. Nichols, who lived next door in a home that would eventually belong to George Cook, took possession of the store in the mid-1900s.

Nancy Phelps Fusco

The Bluebar Oil Company, owned by the Link family, was established in McConnellsville in 1926. It has operated continuously through three generations.

The Har-Phel hydroelectric dam, built by Harley R. Phelps, shown ca. 1920.

The power house with Harley's residence in the background, ca. 1920. Harley R. Phelps built a dam and established an electric company and a spring water system in the early 1920s to service the residents of North Bay. In 1927, he sold the hydroelectric company to what was then the Niagara-Lockport Company. In 1972, his son Russell sold the water business to the town, and a water district was formed.

This is a view of the Phelps factory in 1912.

Har-Phel factory workers included men, women, and an occasional child. They are shown here in 1913; Harley is the taller man in the doorway.

Mauricette TenVooren Sullivan is collecting the sap from sugar maple trees on a Har-Phel farm, ca. 1945.

Barbara (Phelps) Herb and Nancy (Phelps) Fusco are using their best two-hand sap gathering technique.

George Cook is pictured emptying the sap into the collecting container.

After the sap has been filtered, Russell Phelps begins to cook it down into maple syrup.

Ann Hopkins

Lansing Tuttle opened his canning factory in McConnellsville in 1880.

Ann Hopkins

As this can art shows, Tuttle partnered with Theodore Chrestien, and the company grew.

Ann Hopkins

Workers outside the Tuttle Canning Factory prepare corn for canning, ca. 1910.

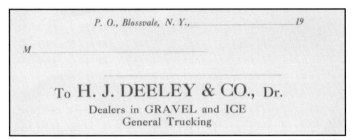

The letterhead of the H.J. Deeley company tells most of the company's story...

... but this picture of "Uncle Harold" Sy Deeley, taken by his niece Ann, gives this trucking company a real image.

Bob Montross

When the railroad depot in North Bay closed in 1934, caretaker agent Jordan sold his coal business to the firm of Collins and Sable, owned by Harold Collins (pictured) and Arthur Sable. This company was allowed in the depot to operate the scales to weigh the coal shipments.

"Skip" Sable

In 1935, Arthur and Esther Sable established a bus company that contracted with the Camden School System.

Dr. Cavana moved to Sylvan Beach from Oneida in 1891 and was a strong influence in the area for the next thirty-three years. He established a sanitarium and a school of nursing and was an active member in local politics. Dr. Cavana helped develop the midway and often backed businesses that were just starting out.

Clayton Montross' home was located west of the garage on Route 49. His son Bob Montross opened a small grocery store, "The Mini Mart," on the same property in 1983. Locals stop by to share a cup of coffee and reminisce a bit with Bob while they pick up a few necessities.

Phoebe Lacell

A combination garage and radio/TV repair formed in 1947 was known as Lacell's Garage. Pete Lacell did all the car repairs while his brother, George, with the help of his wife Lois, sold and repaired radios and TV's. Phoebe kept the books, ran errands, pumped gas and sold groceries. She also relieved Pete for the lunch and supper hours. They originally sold Gulf gasoline and later sold Sunoco. When Route 49 east of Vienna Corners was improved in 1963, the brothers dissolved their partnership. Pete built a garage down the road a bit and George built a TV Sales and Service in the same area; he also sold Scorpion Snowmobiles for a few years. Pete and George both retired in 1987. Pete passed away February 5, 2002, and George passed away April 6, 2005.

HOTELS & RESTAURANTS

Gawers Park, Cabins and Trailer Grounds as they appeared ca. 1930 in Sylvan Beach.

Florence Gawer was the proprietor of the tavern and restaurant, and also the campgrounds.

Walter Richie's hot dog stand was located on the site of the old O&W platform in Sylvan Beach. This photo dates from about 1920.

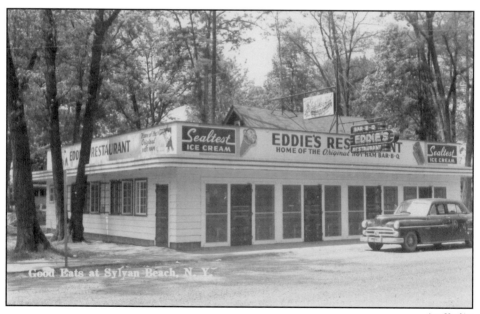

In 1935, Eddie Stewart of Rome bought Walter Richie's hot dog stand. Well-known as the "home of the original hot ham on a toasted bun," Eddie's, shown here ca. 1950, remains a popular restaurant in Sylvan Beach.

In 1927, William H. Murray purchased this building located at the intersection of Routes 49 and 13 in Vienna. He operated it as a grocery store and gas station. In later years, his son James and wife Arlene converted the building into a hotel/restaurant and lived upstairs. In 1962, the hotel was removed to allow the reconstruction of Route 13.

Ann Hopkins

Prior to 1900, North Bay had become a bustling village with around seven hotels. Josiah Cleveland built the North Bay Hotel, also known at one time as the Central Hotel. It was the largest and is the only one that remains today. It is located at the corner of Route 49 and West Lake Street.

The Butler House, near the railroad tracks at the end of West Lake St., North Bay, was built and run by George Butler. The hotel was struck by lightning and burned to the ground. It was never rebuilt.

Horton's original hotel burned on June 26, 1908. It was rebuilt and became a popular gathering place for those waiting for the train, as pictured above in 1919.

In about 1925, the second Horton Hotel was expanded, and eventually it was sold to Charles and Emma Strader. Here is Strader's popular hotel, restaurant and gas station in 1933.

H.J. Myer built the first hotel in North Bay (the tall building in the back on the left side). The hotel housed a ticket agent and waiting room for the railroad until a station was built. The building near the hotel on the right is the railroad station and on the far right are the buildings belonging to the Albert Annis Boat Works.

The Earl Cottage, built in the early 1900s, was owned by Howie Earl Field. Arthur and Esther Sable bought the home and property in 1946 or 1947. In the 1950s, they opened a restaurant that offered fine dining; it operated for ten to fifteen years. Called the Casa Loma (shown in 1922), it is just below the cemetery on West Lake Street, North Bay.

The Paddock House, or Vanden Heuvel Building, ca. 1920. This was an apartment building and also housed businesses. After his store burned in 1887, Henry Woodard moved his business to the east end of this building; the double doors on the end are the entrance to Arthur Cheny's bakery.

Lyman Spencer, son of James D. Spencer (1813–1899), built the first public house in Sylvan Beach, the Forest Home Hotel, in 1879. James Spencer made it his residence.

In the latter 1800s Bill McArthur (center) built a hotel in Jewell. He operated it for many years, an example of the effect of the railroad on local enterprise.

The Jewell Hotel in 1906

The Brigham family and P.J. Sullivan owned and operated the Oneida Lake Club (shown in 1928), a resort hotel in Jewell. The annual fee for membership was ten dollars, and a popular feature was the fresh produce grown on site. The garden and grounds were tended by Dick Kinney.

At the turn of the century Herman Bridenbecker owned the Vienna Hotel, located on the corner of Routes 13 and 49 in Vienna. At around 3:00 A.M. on Sunday, September 3, 1914, the hotel caught fire. Awakened by their dog, the family escaped without injury. Those responding to the alarm were able to remove most of the items on the first floor, but the building was a total loss. In December of the same year, Herman engaged Charles Roswon to build a fireproof hotel on the same site. Today, Jim Ott owns and operates the hotel.

The Park View Hotel in Sylvan Beach was owned by Mr. Gaiser until the early 1940s, when it was sold to Joseph Palmon. For many years, the restaurant and tavern were popular spots for both visitors and locals. Around 1960, it was torn down to make way for the new bridge to cross the Barge Canal.

ROVER, THE MAIL CARRIER

PARK VIEW HOTEL
C. R. SHAW, PROP.
SYLVAN BEACH, N. Y.

Ann Hopkins

Surely someone will recall seeing Rover, the mail carrier of the Park View Hotel.

Ann Hopkins

Hotel Leland was established in 1896 by Charles Scovile. It was later named Hotel Klippel, after the man who purchased it from Scovile.

Klippel moved his building north and changed the name to the Lake Shore Hotel.

The Algonquin Hotel was the first large resort in Sylvan Beach. Built in 1884 by William Rubles for C.G.W. Stoddard and Anthony T. Garvin, it partially burned in 1899. It was completely destroyed by fire in 1904.

The Sylvan Home was subsequently known as the Knickerbocker and Tabarrini's Lodge. It was located on the site which has become Harpoon Eddie's.

The most elaborate of all the hotels in Sylvan Beach was the St. Charles. Built in 1899 and lavishly maintained by Mr. Cheesebrough, it burned in 1914.

Hotel Nobles in Sylvan Beach, 1916. In 1920, William Russell opened Russell's Hotel in the building previously known as Hotel Nobles. After his death, Russell's Danceland became a popular spot during the big band era, featuring the best in entertainment. Bands like Benny Goodman, Paul Whitman, Duke Ellington, Harry James, Glen Miller and Jimmy Dorsey appeared there. When Glen Miller played, the crowd was so large the traffic on Route 13 was backed up for three to four miles south of Sylvan Beach. In later years, the old building became a roller skating rink. The name "Skate Land" brings back pleasant childhood memories for many people.

FIRE & STORM DAMAGE

A fire in "The Beach" tries to take the Forest Home Hotel in 1912.

On July 30, 1912, Sylvan Beach was devastated by fire. Although many businesses were damaged and many more were lost, the Forest Home Hotel was one that survived the disaster.

Destructive Wind Storm at Sylvan Beach, N. Y., April 23, 1912.

This destructive wind storm at Sylvan Beach in 1912 reminds us that in a matter of moments, Oneida Lake can turn from calm to treacherous.

Breaking Up of the Ice on Oneida Lake, Sylvan Beach, N. Y.

Ice on Oneida Lake provided income for ice cutters, and the product of their labor was shipped as far away as Albany. Ice fishing was income for some and sport for others. Sometimes in the spring, when the ice begins to break and pile on the shore, people hear the "thunder" from miles away.

Breaking up of Ice on Oneida Lake, March 1914, Sylvan Beach, N. Y.

Ice breakup on Oneida Lake at Sylvan Beach

Clarence Harden

"An early morning thunder and lightning storm in July 1951 was followed by two and a half hours of heavy rain, causing devastation in much of the countryside and hamlets in the Town of Vienna." In McConnellsville, "The culvert east of the four corners was clogged, so the water overflowed and ran down the hill, washing out nearly all the road between Harden's store and factory."

Journal of a Village, McConnellsville, N.Y. 1828–1970
by Clarence C. Harden

Clarence Harden

"The dirt and debris carried by the rushing water were deposited in the yard of the little house at the bottom of the hill. There was no electricity for nearly twenty-four hours and the factory was closed temporarily."

Journal of a Village, McConnellsville, N.Y. 1828—1970
by Clarence C. Harden

Dibbletown suffered severe damage when a twenty-foot section of Rt. 13 was washed away.

In Jewell, the Hall Brook Bridge on Route 49 washed out when the Claude Harris Dam (on right) failed, taking out the bridge on the Jewell-Camden highway and gouging out large sections of the road.

Rita Fern

The Murray Brook Dam in 1951

The Murray Brook Dam on Route 49 held, but the rushing water and the debris the brook carried ate away at the embankment supporting the bridge, causing it to collapse.

At the H.R. Phelps Factory power house, the back wall is torn away, and a newly installed oil-fired boiler lays at the edge of the stream. The flood water in its course was confronted by the Phelps Dam, which also held. Instead, the water spilled over the west embankment, washing it away. At high flood stage, the water also took out the Phelps Bridge in the valley.

East Lake Street in North Bay is confronted with the flood of 1951.

The bridge connecting West Lake Street to East Lake Street washed out. West Lake Street is shown with the railroad station in the background.

A section of the railroad tracks remained suspended in midair.

A large section of the O&W railroad bed was washed away, leaving the tracks suspended in midair and causing a delay in service on the line. Here, men are working to repair the damage. The bridge on Lake Shore Drive (not pictured) was weakened, making it unsafe for use. With no power or telephone and the bridges washed out, North Bay was left isolated from the rest of the world.

Murray Brook rushes below the weakened Route 49 bridge.

A dry dam after the flood of 1951

Repair poles bridge a calm Murray Brook.

Rebuilding the Rt. 49 bridge at Murray Brook

The new culvert and bridge under construction

The new Rt. 49 bridge is completed at Murray Brook, North Bay.

Roads, Bridges, Rails & Canals

Ann Hopkins

While automobiles were causing astonished stares elsewhere, a surrey and a horse were a common sight in Sylvan Beach in 1900.

Bob Montross

This photo was taken from the curve looking down "Lake Hill" on the south end of West Lake Street in North Bay. Butler House is on the left, a few lots up the hill. At the bottom of the hill is the first railroad station in North Bay, built by the New York & Oswego Midland Railroad in 1869. Myer's Grove is on the left at the bottom of the hill in the valley, and Horton's Tourist Homes are on the right.

West Lake Street in North Bay. Notice that the poles for the electric wires rise only about fifteen feet above the ground.

The Wood River pedestrian and wagon bridge at Sylvan Beach opened in the spring of 1889. Before it was built, the only way across Wood River was by boat.

Part of the Barge Canal Project, this bridge was built just to the west of the old bridge over Wood River. Contracted to Chesley, Earl, Heimback. Inc. in 1917, it cost $9,643.

"The Fish Creek Landing Bridge" (next page), written by Cliff Collins ca. 1985, shows the esteem people have held for the rural ways of earlier Vienna generations.

The Fish Creek Landing Bridge
by Clifton Collins

A happening took place
In nineteen hundred and nine
Few people now remaining
Can remember that time.

The Vienna Town Officials
Worked out a good deal,
And bought a new bridge
Constructed all of steel.

To replace a wooden bridge
Erected many years before
Spanning old Fish Creek
From Cook Road to the General Store.

The bridge was good
In many ways,
But twas built back
In the horse & buggy days.

The floor of the bridge
Was made of plank
And when they dried out
It would rattle and clank.

The ones that designed the bridge
Overlooked one factor,
The effect of vibration caused
By passing truck and tractor.

In nineteen seventy-two
Hurricane Agnes caused a flood,
That greatly weakened the old bridge,
But it the flood withstood.

The Highway Corp of Engineers
Came and took one look
Then they put a new bridge
On their project book.

Our county legislator worked at it
For quite a few years
And finally got approval
Of the project from his peers.

Now the bridge is in a new location
That connects Vienna and Higginsville Roads
It's a real sturdy structure
Designed to carry heavy loads.

They completed the bridge
In the summer of Eighty-four
And each time I travel over it
I appreciate it more and more.

When you come down from Vienna
And drive up over the ridge
You will see a new sign
Inscribed "Earl S. Angell" Bridge.

They dismantled the old bridge
And had it hauled away
But the people who live at the landing
Will remember it for many a day.

Many a saga is preserved in verse and song
As perhaps this one will be
But regardless of what has transpired
A page is turned in History.

O&W Engine #307 is on the siding at the North Bay station.

Donald Muir (left) and Russell Phelps, age 15 or 16, took the train to Oneida to attend high school in 1926.

Railroad Bridge number 367 on Wood River went into service in April of 1887. The bridge is located just west of where Fish Creek and Wood Creek join to form Wood River.

Ann Hopkins

The New York, Ontario & Western Railway Station in North Bay is shown ca. 1920. On May 21, 1878, the first railroad station here was struck by lightning and burned to the ground. This station replaced the previous one and was completed in October of the same year. Located between Oneida Lake and the Murray Creek valley in North Bay, the tracks ran closer to the lake here than at any other point on the line. Eventually the name of the railroad was shortened to the O&W. When business dwindled, many referred to the line as "the Old and Weary."

Sitting on the roof of the New York, Ontario & Western Railway Depot in Sylvan Beach in 1906 are (from left to right): Charles Bouneau, Joe Dixon, Bob Harding, and Clarence Ingersoll, who was the agent at Bernhard's Bay. During the era of train service to Sylvan Beach, multiple stations were built, dismantled and relocated. This was true for both the O&W and the Lehigh railroads; one station was dismantled twice. The summer of 1923 was the last year the O&W station operated on a seasonal schedule and also the last year the depot would occupy its original site. The O&W station in Sylvan Beach shut down September 1, 1934.

This New York & Oswego Midland Railroad depot at Jewell was built between 1869 and 1873. The company was later reorganized as the New York, Ontario & Western Railway. Clinton Drum was the last rail master in Jewell.

The O&W opened a railroad station among the homes and businesses in the hamlet of Fish Creek in 1869. Fish Creek Station was the end of the line. All vacationers en route to Sylvan Beach and all freight headed north departed from the station. In the spring of 1879 a turntable was installed at the station. In 1886, the name changed to Sylvan Junction for a year. In 1887, it reverted back to Fish Creek Station. The station closed in April 1924.

The Elmira, Cortland & Northern Railroad (EC&N) stations at Vienna and McConnellsville had the same twenty by thirty foot dimensions. The Vienna depot was completed in August 1887 and was located between the freight house and the water tower as shown in the picture. The railroad buildings were separated from the depot by Vienna Rd. and located just south of present-day Rt. 49.

McConnellsville was the last of the Canastota Northern stations to be built (October 1887). Canastota Northern was a subsidiary of the EC&N. The majority of the freight was furniture for shipment from the Harden Furniture Company or hopper cars loaded with sand from Grem's sand pit. Grem's remained one of the principal shippers until the retirement of the railroad in August 1938.

Ann Hopkins
Work on this section of the Barge Canal began in the Town of Vienna at Fish Creek.

Known as the ladder-dredge, bucket-dredge, or elevator-dredge, this machine moved on railroad tracks at Fish Creek.

Construction Work on Barge Canal, Fish Creek, N. Y.

Machines were invented which surmounted some difficulties posed by building the Barge Canal during war time.

Men with horses, mules, picks, and shovels were able to accomplish more than a person could imagine. On May 15, 1918, the incoming water signaled the final work was done.

Here, at the mouth of Wood River where it enters the Barge Canal, part of the Sylvan Beach vista had been changed in 1918. Hotel Leland is on the right on the tip of land, and what appear to be "cribbing" logs are lined up along the shore, with work boats extended across the mouth of the river.

This photo, ca. 1919, gives a good view of the lay of the land before the concrete pier was built.

At Sylvan Beach, ca. 1922, some of the newer barges were self-propelled, but the old wooden barges required a boat to pull or nudge them.

Two dredges, the Oneida and the Oswego, were an essential part of the construction and maintenance of the Barge Canal in the Town of Vienna.

A N.Y. State Barge Canal observation tower was placed near the lake and canal junction. Sylvan Beach grew rapidly after the new bridge and the Barge Canal became a reality. The village quickly replaced Fish Creek as the capital of commerce and tourism in the area.

The new pier promoted tourists' use of the Barge Canal at Sylvan Beach.

RECREATION

Sylvan Beach, ca. 1918

Oneida Lake covers an area of approximately 110 square miles, and is a place for fishing, hunting, boating and swimming. Running east and west, the thumb of the Finger Lakes region, it affects the weather and the lives of Vienna's residents. The character of Sylvan Beach on Oneida Lake has changed frequently as forms of entertainment changed with the times. The carousel remains today, although with different horses. The old roller coaster was removed long ago, the timbers used to frame a house which has since become the Canal View Café. Inside the café are historic photos and artifacts of Vienna's past.

The *Sagamore* was built by the Oneida Lake Transportation Company. It was capable of transporting 600 passengers and was considered one of the grandest ships on Oneida Lake from 1908 to 1917.

The roller coaster with the carousel nearby shows the location of the Luna Park midway after the Barge Canal was built. This view shows how the piers were constructed. Forms are ready to receive the stone that will be dumped into them from barges after they are drawn into position by tug boats like the one in the left foreground. Cement was added later to form the pier that extended out into Oneida Lake. This extended pier created a breakwater so canal users entering the lake would experience fewer side currents.

Ann Hopkins

At Carnival Park's entrance anticipation builds for visitors, as screams which fill the air near the roller coaster are balanced by the sounds of laughter and a merry melody from the carousel.

The Sylvan Beach midway prompted many fun-seeking tourists to visit.

A popular midway ride was the Ocean Wave, ca. 1900.

Two of the many steam-powered excursion boats that carried visitors to the parks and hotels.

The *Gateway* was an inboard excursion boat.

The *Lottie* belonged to the Hotel Leland. Several hotels owned steamers to transport vacationers from the Fish Creek railway station before one was built in "The Beach" in 1886. Steamer traffic was a vital part of life in Sylvan Beach. In July 1910, thirty-five steamers licensed to transport passengers were counted traveling the waters of Oneida Lake.

Brandyann Phelps

The Sylvan Beach carousel's original figures were hand-carved by craftsman Joseph Cottman in 1896. The figures were replaced with horses ca. 1976–77.

Figure 8. Sylvan Beach, N. Y.

Brandyann Phelps

At Carnival Park, Sylvan Beach, there were other games and rides. Here is the roller coaster known as the Figure 8.

Water Toboggan. SYLVAN BEACH, N. Y.

Brandyann Phelps

The Toboggan Slide, erected by George Delong in 1893, was owned by Rosco and Eva Cook in 1900. It entertained generations of teens and adults.

Riding astride at the pony livery in bonnets and long dresses, these young women might have been seen as too daring in any other setting.

The "Penny" Arcade at Sylvan Beach, ca. 1900, offered indoor amusements and shelter from the sun and rain.

The Hop Growers Association held their first picnic in Sylvan Beach in 1878. The number of passengers was so great in 1887 that the O&W was forced to use some freight cars along with all their passenger cars to transport passengers. In 1888, it was said to be "the biggest ever," with ninety-three railroad passenger carloads arriving on the New York, Ontario & Western and forty-six on the Elmira, Cortland & Northern, to make a total of 139 railroad passenger cars. This picture is dated 1890.

Vacationers didn't come to the lake just for the carousels, games and ponies. These camps on Edgewater Beach, ca. 1920, show a peaceful, though congested, side of the area.

In the mid-1870s, the Northern Division Superintendent of the New York & Oswego Midland Railroad, Charles W. Lanpher, insisted that the railroad should build its own picnic grounds at North Bay, where their tracks ran closest to the lake. The result was Myers Grove.

For years, campers and picnickers arrived at Myers Grove, a short walk from the railroad or the North Bay pier, where steamboats docked. This group picture, ca. 1895, (all unnamed) is set among stones which remain to this day.

Jeanne Hatzinger and Anne Teelin

Local townspeople gathered to see this "miracle" of air transportation—the George, Ed and Frank Hatzinger hot air balloons—in Blossvale, 1914.

Bob Montross

Ron Montross, age 13, uses the down-stroke to start the engine on the air ice boat.

Ice sailing on the lake in 1931 required warm clothing and good sailing skills. As a reward, sailors went fast and far across the open spaces.

Lake spray and the wind in your face are thrills many will continue to share while on the waters of Oneida Lake.

BIBLIOGRAPHY

Flagg, Arlene. *History of the Vienna United Methodist Church, Vienna, New York, 1804–2001*. Privately published, 2002.

Harden, Clarence C. *Journal of a Village: McConnellsville, N.Y. 1828–1970*. (As taken from diaries, scrapbooks, histories, and remembrances).

Henke, Jack. *Oneida Lake "The Only Happiness"—Place Names and History*. Utica, New York: North Country Books, 1989.

Henke, Jack. *Sylvan Beach on the Lake Oneida—A History*. Utica, New York: North Country Books, 1975.

Henke, Jack. *Tales of Oneida Lake*. Utica, New York: North Country Books, 1993.

Norton, Mary Clarke. *The Early History of Elpis School District #17. Township of Vienna, Oneida County, N.Y.: Sequel to Whiskey Island School District No. 16*. Unpublished manuscript, 1960.

Norton, Mary Clarke. *The History of Whiskey Island–School District #16. Town of Vienna, Oneida County, New York As I Know It*. Unpublished manuscript, 1954.

Vienna Seventh-Day Adventist Church, 1899–1976. (An illustrated history compiled by church leaders). Self-published, 1976.

White, Donald. *Exploring 200 Years of Oneida County History*. Utica, New York: Oneida County Historical Society, 1988.

Wimmet, Father Leo. *St. John's and St. Mary's Have a History of Progress*. Self-published.